ADRIFT ON A RUBY YACHT

ERIC CHEVLEN

Borromean Books
Youngstown, Ohio

Adrift on a Ruby Yacht. Copyright © 2014, Eric Chevlen.

Permission is granted to copy or reprint portions for any noncommercial use, except they may not be posted online without permission.

ISBN 978-0-9830559-0-7

Library of Congress Control Number: 2013922716

Library of Congress Subject Headings:
    Poetry—21st Century
    Poetry, American

Cover design by Tamara Chevlen.

For Laurel, who doubles my joys, and halves my sorrows.

ADRIFT ON A RUBY YACHT

Preface

All the world's a stage,
And all the men and women merely players:
They have their exits and their entrances;
And one man in his time plays many parts,
His acts being seven ages. At first the infant,
Mewling and puking in the nurse's arms.
And then the whining school-boy, with his satchel
And shining morning face, creeping like snail
Unwillingly to school. And then the lover,
Sighing like furnace, with a woeful ballad
Made to his mistress' eyebrow. Then a soldier,
Full of strange oaths and bearded like the pard,
Jealous in honour, sudden and quick in quarrel,
Seeking the bubble reputation
Even in the cannon's mouth. And then the justice,
In fair round belly with good capon lined,
With eyes severe and beard of formal cut,
Full of wise saws and modern instances;
And so he plays his part. The sixth age shifts
Into the lean and slippered pantaloon,
With spectacles on nose and pouch on side,
His youthful hose, well saved a world too wide
For his shrunk shank; and his big manly voice,
Turning again toward childish treble, pipes
And whistles in his sound. Last scene of all,
That ends this strange eventful history,
Is second childishness and mere oblivion,
Sans teeth, sans eyes, sans taste, sans everything.

—William Shakespeare, *As You Like It*

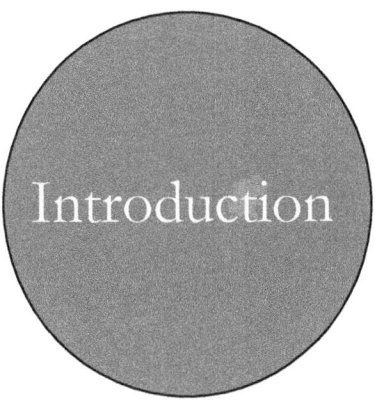

Introduction

Once Shakespeare wrote of mankind's seven ages,
Through which we march as simpletons or sages.
And now I sing of grace which each age brings,
That grace which all our would-be wounds assuages.

ADRIFT ON A RUBY YACHT

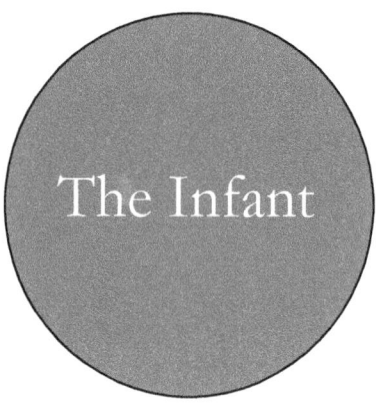

Emerging from the darkness to the light,
The colors! Sounds! The air! Ah, the delight
To see her face, whose voice I'd always loved,
My first, and ever since, most precious sight.

THE INFANT

Into this world of wonder I am placed,
A world of sight and sound and smell and taste,
A world abundant, blessèd, lovely, graced.
O joyous world embracing and embraced!

She drew me nigh, and lay me on her breast;
Her soft and gentle hands in love caressed.
No soul incarnate ever knew more joy,
Nor angel in God's heaven was as blessed.

ADRIFT ON A RUBY YACHT

He does not cease to be when out of view,
But comes back to surprise with joy anew.
I learned of God and Providence quite young,
While playing with my father peek-a-boo.

The steed I rode was really grandpa's knee.
The reins, his fingers clasped exultantly.
The sagebrush smell, cigars and after-shave.
The joy, to give the joy he took in me.

THE INFANT

As twilight swells and day comes to its close,
Before the lullabies and night's repose,
She sponges me in water warm and pure,
And dries and counts and kisses all my toes.

It's not by sun or star or moonlight gleams
We see the world is more than what it seems.
I close my eyes. An inner light reveals
A second virgin world within my dreams.

The Schoolboy

As pigeons flock to feed, at morning bell
We gather 'round our teacher, and the spell
She casts on us will hold us all our lives,
For all of life is naught but show and tell.

THE SCHOOLBOY

The long dead heroes, hailed in song and deed,
Revivified, would come to me and lead
Me to their elsewise hidden treasure-troves,
When I but said the password: I can read.

The arts and music, prose and poetry
Would beckon me, a vaster world to see,
Abundant, overflowing, which imbues
Its grace to life without necessity.

ADRIFT ON A RUBY YACHT

And mathematics, science's true queen,
Demonstrable, inerrant, and pristine,
Would yield quadratic truth at my behest—
Not more, not less, naught else, and naught between.

From year to year, in summer and in snow,
I learned, and felt my knowledge steady grow,
Until, at last, I then began to learn
Those things I didn't know I didn't know.

THE SCHOOLBOY

And as I learned, yet more my knowledge grew,
And so I learned that, far more than I knew,
The world and life is more than I can know,
And stands on truths I cannot know are true.

Though many schools in time I would attend,
And many paths of academe would wend,
I still retain the best of all I gleaned,
That boy, that man, my dear and lifelong friend.

The Lover

Like flowers, schemes may sprout and bloom, then fade
And shrivel, never mind how firmly made,
And go awry, these schemes of mice and men.
Of all my schemes, she was the one best laid.

THE LOVER

And when I press her breasts against my own,
Flesh of her perfumed flesh, bone of my bone,
Like distant tympani we hear increase
Love's rumbling release and passion's moan.

Design divine, beyond all human arts,
Implanted in us interlocking hearts.
Discover heaven! Come with me, my love,
Uncover other interlocking parts.

ADRIFT ON A RUBY YACHT

I knew love at first glance did not belong
Outside of fairy tales and sappy songs,
And knew such glance would never glance my way.
We met. At once I knew I had been wrong.

In gazing in the mirror I would see
That I that I objectified as me,
But now I see reflected in your eyes
Your I and mine united as our we.

THE LOVER

Now past and future meld in love, endow
The present moment rapturous, allow
The two as one, the you and me, to be
Embraced in love in our eternal now.

Through us, with us, our forebears intermesh,
Rejuvenate, invigorate, refresh
And crown those ancient lines with newborn life:
This child, conceived in love, flesh of our flesh.

The Soldier

The soldier for the statesman pays the price,
When nastiness is needed after nice.
Reluctant though I go to war to kill
Or die for country, I would do it twice.

THE SOLDIER

We few, we happy few, we brothers' band,
United, unrequited, and unplanned,
Confront and hunt the foe without reprieve,
Defend our faith, our families, our land.

And so we march, our fate and glory shared,
Where none before prevailed, and few have dared.
Come steel, come stone, come death as flesh and bone,
Come hell's foul breath ablaze—we are prepared.

ADRIFT ON A RUBY YACHT

Come, enemy, you can no longer hide.
Emerge, and join the ranks of those who vied
Against my might. Tonight you sleep in dust—
And I shall speak of how you bravely died.

Perhaps he has a wife. He too may be
The father of two daughters, maybe three,
A decent chap—but one of us must die.
I aim. I shoot. Yes, better him than me.

THE SOLDIER

Anticipated stingless Death, sit here.
Before we wrestle, this I will make clear:
Perhaps you have the pow'r to make me die,
But never nevermore to make me fear.

Like resurrected shades enfleshed anew,
Bewildered and delighted—is it true?—
The war is over! Now we can go home!
Eternal peace? I doubt. But it will do.

The Justice

The common law, constructed case by case,
A marble temple on a granite base,
No one man built, let no man undermine,
As in its priesthood proud I take my place.

THE JUSTICE

By equal law, the greatest and the least
Are tried and judged, imprisoned or released.
No one above, and none beneath the law,
For man is not an angel—nor a beast.

I weigh the law, its spirit and its letter.
Accused and victim, creditor and debtor
Alike in dignity await my word.
Imperfect though I am, none could do better.

ADRIFT ON A RUBY YACHT

The law's concern is torts and crime, not sins
Nor angels pirouetting on gold pins.
When law exceeds these bounds, then justice ends.
When justice ends, then tyranny begins.

The majesty of justice, like a wall,
Forfends the forces furious which call
For anarchy, the end of which would be
Unending war of all avenging all.

THE JUSTICE

The common law from case to case may grow,
And legislatures statutes may bestow,
But natural unchanging laws perdure,
The laws which mankind cannot cannot know.

And I too shall be judged some Judgment Day
For everything I've said and didn't say,
And all my deeds, before a higher court.
Come judge me, Judge, and rule! I shall obey.

The Slippered Pantaloon

The sun arose, the bridegroom from his tent,
And strode the stretched ecliptic firmament
In majesty, while all that day I basked,
Nor ever lived a day more richly spent.

THE SLIPPERED PANTALOON

My children seek advice they will not take,
Then scamper off to make the same mistake
That oft I made when I was young like them.
With luck I have a few still left to make.

Who is this man the mirror shows to me,
This wrinkle-faced reflection that I see?
That I can see!—I see that I can see,
And yet may be full all that I may be!

ADRIFT ON A RUBY YACHT

Youth's florid flush of passion may subside,
But faith and hope and love—these three abide
As side by side we share our breath abed,
Our passion less expressed, but more implied.

No more the dupe of promises and lies,
No more a prey to wolves in wool disguise,
My eyes are open now; I clearly see.
The years that made me wary made me wise.

THE SLIPPERED PANTALOON

The rivers where I waded still entice
And call to mind the ancient Greek advice,
Which happily is also true of books:
You cannot dip into the same one twice.

Embrace! Farewell—and no regretful thought,
And pray I leave as much as I have brought,
For whither spirit blows, to there I sail.
The cord is cut—adrift on a ruby yacht!

Sans Everything

Some deaths are likened to a bristled burr
Drawn from a throat—perhaps that will occur—
And others to a hair drawn out of milk.
In either case—but briefly to endure.

SANS EVERYTHING

A drop of water dropped into the sea
Is indistinct, but does not cease to be.
A buried seed will sprout with next year's crop—
And I anticipate no less for me

No more to hear the breakers pound the shoal.
No more to hear the melancholy toll
Of mourning bells. I hear no more. But hark!
Attend: the quiet murmur of my soul.

ADRIFT ON A RUBY YACHT

Those days have blown when I would fly a kite,
Hold tightly, steady lift it out of sight,
Then cut the straining string between my teeth.
Now fly! Now fly untethered without bite!

When formerly I had the gift to see,
I saw what was, but not what yet might be.
Be gone, mundane distractions and deceit!
O shine, eternal light, O shine on me!

SANS EVERYTHING

I would not tarry more, were I to eat.
My whole life I've consumed, so why repeat?
It's carnival! Farewell, we say, to flesh.
Who needs no flesh, he surely needs no meat.

No fleshy fetters hobble you and cling.
Arise, O breathless soul, arise and sing
In exultation rapturous and pure,
Sans teeth, sans eyes, sans taste, sans everything!

Adrift on a Ruby Yacht

Adrift on a Ruby Yacht

Adrift on a Ruby Yacht

SANS EVERYTHING

These people gathered 'round me are not here,
But conjured by my mind, to disappear
Along with me as soon I breathe my last,
The vapor of indifference, not fear.

The toll is rung which no one can unring.
The dirge is sung which no one can unsing.
Now go back whence you came before your birth,
Sans teeth, sans eyes, sans taste, sans everything.

ADRIFT ON A RUBY YACHT

Predictably surprising: to grow old,
To sense our senses slipping from our hold.
Unwonted and unwanted, touch persists,
The least that lasted last—but oh so cold!

As toothless as the worms which lie in wait,
I lie and wait the advent of my fate
Expected, hooking me yet unaware.
It comes so soon—and yet it comes so late.

SANS EVERYTHING

Like dreams, like shadows misty and obscure,
Like memory of thoughts that never were,
The images of life in shades of gray
Dissolve and disappear into a blur.

The buzzing, hums, and chirpings may abound
In this stale world, but not beneath the mound
Where, there and then, as here and now, we'll lie
Bereft of sight and smell and taste and sound.

ADRIFT ON A RUBY YACHT

My days for looking forward are long past.
My vision, like my days, is fading fast.
I sense the inky blackness seeping in,
Until the feeble flame be snuffed at last.

THE SLIPPERED PANTALOON

No longer do I miss a furtive kiss,
The clash of arms, or standing up to piss.
Desire itself no longer within reach,
I miss the missing all I used to miss.

From there to here, from birth to pending rot,
I sail these seven seas in stillborn thought
Of then, and now, and when, and how, and why,
Unmoored, alone, adrift on a ruby yacht.

ADRIFT ON A RUBY YACHT

The pretty girls rush by and do not pause
To stop to say hello, perhaps because
The time they have is not the same as mine.
Their time now is "I am," and mine—"I was."

Not loved, perhaps, but surely I was kissed.
If not caressed, at least I felt a fist.
But now, unseen, untouched, I haunt this world,
And wonder: do I truly still exist?

THE SLIPPERED PANTALOON

Each day do I deplete my daily store
Of hoped-for days to do the deeds I swore
That I would do before I die. And worse:
How many deeds I shall do—nevermore!

Returning to my haunts where formerly
I earned my share of notoriety,
I barely recognize the place at all.
I know nobody here—and none knows me.

ADRIFT ON A RUBY YACHT

The Slippered Pantaloon

In foolish youth, my aspirations hung
Just out of reach. Not old enough, I clung
To the belief that time was on my side.
Now naught remains for which I am too young.

THE JUSTICE

Some judges take the offered bribe, and whore
Themselves in shame, but I refuse. I swore
An oath to guard my honor and the law's.
Insulting fools, they should have offered more.

Although the law is iron, I adjust
It to the circumstances as I must
To reach the verdict I have foreordained.
The law is born as iron, dies as rust.

ADRIFT ON A RUBY YACHT

The majesty of law brooks no delay,
Compelling all before us to obey,
And cases which have languished now for years
Will also come to us—but not today.

We wear black robes of justice but to hide
The blacker blackness crouched within, inside
The human hearts whence leaps the force of law,
Which if the people knew, would not abide.

THE JUSTICE

The lawyers strut, gesticulate, exhort
Their client's claim for justice from my court,
But here I am the law, and I will choose
Which rascal will his fellow's wealth extort.

When Law conflicts with Justice, which to choose?
And shall I rule in candor or by ruse?
Or should I flip a coin to judge the case
Of Law v. Justice. Heads or tails, we lose.

ADRIFT ON A RUBY YACHT

The Justice

If governance be more than power raw,
The justice must his due distinction draw
In calibration measured to effect:
Who is above, and who beneath the law?

THE SOLDIER

With ink and paper diplomats suspend
Hostilities, and toast to warfare's end.
The soldier writes his fate with blood and mud,
And wonders who is foe and who is friend.

Here lies my fallen comrade, laid to rest
In this neglected grave—he was the best
And bravest soldier, dying in my stead—
While here lies this bright medal on my chest.

ADRIFT ON A RUBY YACHT

If I should fall, then plant me six feet deep,
And swear to me one promise you must keep,
The only thing I've craved for all these years:
Alive or dead or both—just let me sleep.

As he lay dying, felled by my own hand,
He beckoned me draw nigh to listen, and
I heard his final gasped and gurgled words,
But what he said, I could not understand.

THE SOLDIER

The enemy approaches, and too late
The soldier recognizes him as Fate,
Intemperate and merciless and swift,
Refusing pleas to linger or to wait.

A captive of the enemy, I peer
Between these bars to see his mocking leer
Contemptuous. Ah well I know that face,
As well I know my own. His name is Fear.

ADRIFT ON A RUBY YACHT

The Soldier

When I was young, in uniform, and I
Was told that I must kill or I must die,
I made the choice that soldiers ever make.
I don't regret my choice, but don't know why.

THE LOVER

In searching and researching under cover
To learn the mysteries of love and lover,
I came to know, though not the first or last,
No mysteries remain me to discover.

That love is not true love unless it burn
Afar as brightly as at hand. I learn
A distant blaze may give off sparks, ignite
A distant pyre—and she will not return.

ADRIFT ON A RUBY YACHT

I worshipped every hair upon her head,
Each florid breath, each word of love she said.
But breath, like words, like evanescent love,
Like hair, springs from the living—but is dead.

Betimes when other arms or legs would tempt
This flesh, which from temptation's not exempt,
This flesh to yielding flesh would soon subside.
The passion, too, subsided—to contempt.

THE LOVER

We spoke, in all the innocence of youth,
Of faithfulness, and love, and patient ruth.
So many tender words! But these remain:
"Though honesty I love; I hate the truth."

Again and yet again flesh hunger led
Me eager, if not earnest, to her bed.
How long I craved, how briefly satisfied
That hunger which but grows, the more it's fed!

ADRIFT ON A RUBY YACHT

The Lover

She loves me not—she loves me—loves me not.
Her love is freely given—rented—bought.
Both paramour and paradox is she,
So cold at times—yet even then, so hot!

THE SCHOOLBOY

A rainbow is the symbol, ever plain,
That God will not destroy the world again.
I saw my first while walking home from school.
Behind, the sun; ahead of me, the rain.

Perhaps a ray of light once pierced my pall.
Perhaps I sipped on nectar once, not gall.
What difference now, so many years have passed?
That youth is dead, whose life I can't recall.

ADRIFT ON A RUBY YACHT

The bigger boys, the stronger boys and tall
Would duly dole my daily dose of gall,
Humiliation I could not outgrow,
So even when I grew, I still was small.

In scholarship, competing tooth and nail
Against my rivals, hoping to prevail
In just one thing, I learned of work's reward:
With work I might succeed—or still might fail.

THE SCHOOLBOY

Consigned to school, I learned on my first day
Where I must sit or stand, but must not pray.
I learned I must not speak if not my turn,
But most of all I learned: I must obey.

In sports I was a loser, far out-classed
By boys who could hit harder and run fast,
But still they always chose me for their team.
They chose me for their team—but always last.

ADRIFT ON A RUBY YACHT

The Schoolboy

A child has so many things to learn,
Like who will love him true, and who will spurn.
My father taught that lesson to me well,
The day he left us, never to return.

THE INFANT

Though wordless, I could cry, oh I could cry
For help from those alone who could supply
Fulfillment of my cravings and my needs,
Which soon I learned they also could deny.

In love she offered me her turgid tit,
In mother's love, for all I knew of it,
And hungrily I sucked, and still regret
That toothless though I was, I also bit.

ADRIFT ON A RUBY YACHT

Two voices cry in pain and intertwine;
The pain of birth and that of life combine.
One voice I'd heard, though distant, all my life.
The other voice, a stranger's: it was mine!

At birth, as at our death, the way is shut
To going back, and each one wonders what
Could justify our lonely sojourn here.
At death, as at our birth, the cord is cut.

THE INFANT

Not last night, but at night my life began
In passion of a woman and a man,
But now that passion, like my life, is spent
Long since, bereft of purpose or of plan.

In passion or deceit we are conceived,
Or both, if ever passion is believed,
But both to sad indifference decline,
And, lies or love, we're equally deceived.

ADRIFT ON A RUBY YACHT

The Infant

A slimy thing, my tiny fingers curled
Into a fist of protest, I was hurled
From darkness warm into a darkness cold,
And, causing pain, blood-smeared, came to the world.

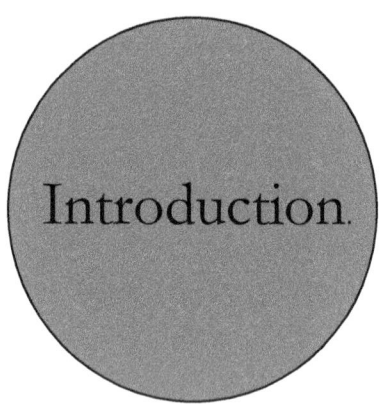

Introduction.

Once Shakespeare wrote of mankind's seven ages,
And now I write of them, the soul that rages,
A prisoner in flesh who can't escape,
Dear hearts who beat in vain against our cages.

ADRIFT ON A RUBY YACHT

Preface

All the world's a stage,
And all the men and women merely players:
They have their exits and their entrances;
And one man in his time plays many parts,
His acts being seven ages. At first the infant,
Mewling and puking in the nurse's arms.
And then the whining school-boy, with his satchel
And shining morning face, creeping like snail
Unwillingly to school. And then the lover,
Sighing like furnace, with a woeful ballad
Made to his mistress' eyebrow. Then a soldier,
Full of strange oaths and bearded like the pard,
Jealous in honour, sudden and quick in quarrel,
Seeking the bubble reputation
Even in the cannon's mouth. And then the justice,
In fair round belly with good capon lined,
With eyes severe and beard of formal cut,
Full of wise saws and modern instances;
And so he plays his part. The sixth age shifts
Into the lean and slippered pantaloon,
With spectacles on nose and pouch on side,
His youthful hose, well saved a world too wide
For his shrunk shank; and his big manly voice,
Turning again toward childish treble, pipes
And whistles in his sound. Last scene of all,
That ends this strange eventful history,
Is second childishness and mere oblivion,
Sans teeth, sans eyes, sans taste, sans everything.

—William Shakespeare, *As You Like It*

For Laurel, who halves my sorrows and doubles my joys.

Adrift on a Ruby Yacht. Copyright © 2014, Eric Chevlen.

Permission is granted to copy or reprint portions for any
noncommercial use, except they may not be posted online without
permission.

ISBN 978-0-9830559-0-7

Library of Congress Control Number: 2013922716

Library of Congress Subject Headings:
    Poetry—21st Century
    Poetry, American

Cover design by Tamara Chevlen.

ADRIFT ON A RUBY YACHT

ERIC CHEVLEN

Borromean Books
Youngstown, Ohio

www.ingramcontent.com/pod-product-compliance
Lightning Source LLC
Chambersburg PA
CBHW031214090426
42736CB00009B/908